# Love Ideas
## in
## Covid Pandemic Times

For Couples & Lovers

CHARLES MWEWA

Ottawa, 2021

Copyright © 2021 Charles Mwewa

All rights reserved.

ISBN: 978-1-988251-36-3

## DEDICATION

To couples and lovers worldwide.

## CONTENTS

DEDICATION ......................................................... iii
CONTENTS .............................................................. v
AUTHOR'S WORD ................................................. vi
1 LOVE DESPITE FEAR ......................................... 1
2 DEATH IS INEVITABLE ...................................... 3
3 MAKE A LOCKDOWN A LOVE HAVEN ..... 5
4 SPEAK THE HOPE OF TOMORROW ............ 7
5 LIVE LOVE IN THE MOMENT ...................... 11
6 FOCUS ON YOUR LOVER .............................. 13
7 DINE TOGETHER OFTEN .............................. 15
8 CULTIVATE INTIMACY ................................... 19
9 FINE-TUNE YOUR LOVE LANGUAGE ..... 27
10 MAKE LOVE OFTEN ...................................... 33
INDEX ..................................................................... 37
ABOUT THE AUTHOR ...................................... 40

## AUTHOR'S WORD

The Covid-19 pandemic has not just been about the saddest period of modern human history, but also the loneliest for couples and lovers. Each day, all they read, hear and listen to, are sad stories and bad news of rising infections and death.

And in such times, love may be thrown out of the window. But it shouldn't. Lovers and couples can live these moments in bliss. They can love more, feel for each other more, and give more to their relationships.

This little book is for all lovers and couples in the Covid-pandemic times. It will stimulate them towards increased desire for one another, and it will give them the encouragement to continue to live and love. There is no balm as healing as love, and no antidote most effective against death as love.

*Love word for this Chapter* _____.

"Perfect love casts out fear," – Bible,
1 John 4:18

## 1 LOVE DESPITE FEAR

The world is at a precipice of faith and fear. With each day's news bringing nothing but fear – fear of being close, of not being infected, and affected, and fear that a loved one might be next to succumb – people are living on the edge. In such times, it is possible that one's love relationships may suffer. Neglect with excuse may be the order of the day. Couples may feel that "the other will understand" if they do not love as always.

However, the pandemic with its waves and lockdowns may just be the best place to nurture and cultivate your love life. Before Covid, and perhaps at its outset, your relationship might have been good. Now it is time to make it better.

Turn fear into faith – and believe that now is the opportune moment to shower your love life with that closeness you had coveted in pre-Covid times.

You can seize the moment. This time, the object of your love is right there, always. Make them feel safe in your presence, at least, they will feel that you care despite the bad news in the world. Make them your world and in your world, they matter most. You can do this by embracing what is common between you, such as you all are at home or are "locked-up." So, bring yourselves together for a movie night, dining together and wherever permitted, taking small walks together (with masks on, of course, to protect others).

Love conquers all fear.

*Love word for this Chapter* _____.

"Death leaves a heartache no one can heal; love leaves a memory no one can steal" – From an Irish Headstone

## 2 DEATH IS INEVITABLE

Death may be inevitable but love conquers death. During the Covid pandemic, death is the first and last news item on TV, radios and even in newspapers. The first news aired is usually the number of people who got infected or died that day.

And there will be death in many homes. Some of those who will die are lovers. For some, it could be the last time you are being together as a couple. Therefore, take this time to be good to each other. And this is not just because one of you may die, it is because it is the best thing to do. If you can, avoid quarrels and misunderstandings. Live in harmony and say those words that you had not said in pre-Covid times. You know that it could be the end of your partner's life. So, satisfy them. Make them feel loved and keep on doing that every day.

When death comes, it should find nothing that you both regret. It should find two undaunted lovers who are able to stay together in death or in life. And if death should claim one of you, the remaining partner will have good memories of the other.

This may seem to be obvious, but nothing is to be taken for granted during periods of great perturbations like the Covid-19 pandemic. People are dying and one of them can be you. Don't let death defeat your love; rather, remain true to your lover even in the face of death. Don't give death a chance to make you sad. There will always be death – and so, too, is life afterwards. So, be vigilant and don't let death deter you from loving the one who matters most in your life.

If you are married, you promised each other to be there for each other "till death do us part." Now that death is staring the world in its face, dare not to deviate from that promise. If you are still together, in your home or at the hospital, it is an opportunity to show that you care and deeply love each other. Others may not be that fortunate to be together due to Covid restrictions. But even to those who may not be together, a good thought of each other during the pandemic time, is a great thing. Love conquers death.

*Love word for this Chapter* _____.

"Two men look out [from] the same prison bars; one sees mud and the other stars," – Beck

### 3 MAKE A LOCKDOWN A LOVE HAVEN

To curb the spread of Covid-19, many governments recommended lockdowns and imposed stay-at-home orders. It was also reported that during those lockdowns, a heightened level of depression and relationship break-ups threatened marriages and families.

You get the point – depression, stress and family break-ups will be things of the past if lovers choose to embrace the moment. Lockdowns should not be causes of depression and distress. Rather, these should be moments lovers fall in love with each other all over. The obstacles which prevented their love from blossoming are now out of the way. Jobs, businesses and outside activities have been limited by lockdown measures. Couples and lovers can now find themselves spending more time together. They can use this time to cultivate love, and to bond.

Couples and lovers should lock themselves in the bond of love. They should not let the lockdown be their prison. But they should turn it into a paradise. Yes, they should insist on being happy, of being stubbornly and insanely happy.

Let love thrive in the lockdown.

*Love word for this Chapter* _____.

"Learn from yesterday, live for today, hope for tomorrow. The important thing is not to stop questioning," – Albert Einstein

## 4 SPEAK THE HOPE OF TOMORROW

Hope wins. Eventually, the pandemic will pass. But not before it wreaks havoc in the world. Give hope to your spouse or lover. Let them know that no matter what happens, their tomorrow is a bright one. Do not despair and lose hope. Rather, energize your spouse or lover with a breath of warmth and the soothing of kind words.

In some countries, the pandemic has also brought other openings. Some in pre-Covid times, due to busy schedules and a never-ending cycle of activities, had given up on their hobbies and other pursuits. Others had postponed completing their education or advancing their career goals. Well, the pandemic could be a good place to continue, to rekindle the passion and finish a mission.

Find an online course you can do. Participate in remote learning or even complete a diploma, a degree or take graduate studies. During the pandemic, engage in activities that will make your post-Covid pandemic world worthwhile. You don't want to get to the other side the same struggling-you. You don't want to retain the same unprofitable position, the same unsatisfactory job or the same meagre salary. You want to emerge stronger and be in a position that strengthens your resolve.

In post-Covid times, new opportunities will come. New jobs will be created and new adventures will present themselves. If you had prepared during the lockdown and in stay-at-home times, you would face the post-Covid era with confidence. If you had done nothing, at best, you would return to your pre-Covid routines, and at worst, you would be left out of the new adventures.

You can speak to the hope of tomorrow by being smart during the Covid pandemic times. Invest in the available time – so that when times start to move again, you will be ready. Don't procrastinate; don't postpone good ideas and good actions.

Ease on drinking, smoking and other vulnerable habits. The lockdowns can be very tempting moments. Some people may be spending unending-times on Netflix and playing video games. Live life in moderation even during the Covid lockdowns. You can still enjoy life while being responsible and thoughtful of the future. When the Covid pandemic comes to an end, you should emerge stronger, a winner and a better person than before the pandemic.

There is hope for tomorrow. There is a brilliant world out there, after Covid. Life will surely return to normal. Life will be grand again – and normalcy as people knew it pre-Covid, will return. But before it does, live with hope.

People should not lose the hope of tomorrow for today's troubles. They should not lose today's joys for the fear of tomorrow, either. Even in the midst of the Covid pandemic, there are flashes of inspiration and moments of love. People should choose to love and be inspired by acts of courage and sacrifice.

Jonas Salk said, "Hope lies in dreams, in imagination, and in the courage of those who dare to make dreams into reality." Indeed, the devastations of Covid-19, even at their worst, cannot compare to the blissful future that awaits. The sorrow of today will have a clear morning tomorrow. The losses of today will be the seeds through which the harvest of tomorrow will be gathered. If the world does not lose hope now, it will reap healing, joy and happiness tomorrow.

Lovers and couples should learn to believe – to hope in the beautiful future of their relationship as they embrace and enjoy every present joy.

When lovers hope, they turn the tides of hopelessness against the gory veneer of the pandemic. They remain true to their course and do not whimper with the fatal sting of Covid-19.

The Creator agrees, there is hope in your tomorrow. Jeremiah 29:11 says, "'For I know the plans I have for you,' declares the LORD, 'plans to…give you hope and a future.'"

Hope grants love eternal.

*Love word for this Chapter* _____.

"Don't quit. Suffer now and live the rest of your life as a champion," – Muhammad Ali

"True, we love life, not because we are used to living, but because we are used to loving. There is always some madness in love, but there is also always some reason in madness," – Petrarch

## 5 LIVE LOVE IN THE MOMENT

The moment to love is now. Perhaps in pre-Covid period you were kept away from your lover or spouse. You rarely had time for each other. You were always busy or you were overtaken by all the busyness of life. You had lost track. You could even have neglected your partner. Perhaps, without the fault of yours. Or you found yourself falling for another woman, another man. Or you had begun to regret, or even to envy other couples.

Well, the time has presented itself for you to love again. Don't live with regrets. Don't live in fear. Don't live wondering what could have been. Instead, live love in the moment. Find creative ways to satisfy your lover or spouse. Find small things to do together or by yourself and surprise your lover or spouse.

For the most part, if you are going to successfully live love in the moment, you must forgive the past pre-Covid-19 mistakes of your partner. Try to see them in a new light. Try to imagine the good times together, and then action them. Yes, you can. You can spontaneously trigger love. You can be the first to begin the love routine; the love beat.

Don't hate. Don't remember the old wounds. Don't dwell on frustrations or the bad news of the time. Acknowledge all the bad news going around you. Then ignore them. If just for this moment. Find time to embrace, to hug, to kiss, and yes, even to make love.

When the world is reeling from the loss of loved ones, and you still have your partner with you, why don't you be grateful to God and embrace them? Why don't you tell them that you love them, you appreciate them and you are proud of them? Why don't you buy them a gift, a small gift, to remind them that they matter in this moment? Why don't you consult your creative self and use it to ingratiate yourself to your partner? Why don't you live love in this moment? Please do.

Live love, now.

*Love word for this Chapter* _____.

"Love is a game that two can play and both win," – Eva Gabor

6 FOCUS ON YOUR LOVER

When the world is busy focusing on the pandemic, focus on your spouse, your lover. Do not neglect them. Do not give them a chance to resort to childish behaviors like pornography or masturbation. Be there for them. Be sensitive to their needs.

During the pre-pandemic times, most couples focused on their jobs or on themselves. They gave excuses for love. Love had become an inconvenience or an endurance.

But during the Covid pandemic, make your lover your priority number one. Devote time and energy to them. Make their desires your desire, their needs your needs. If you give love, you will reap love. If you give hate, you will, in turn, be hated. If you allow negligence, you will be neglected.

Today, love your lover deeply. Focus only on their interests. Be prescient; concentrate on their best end. If you have to do something to win them back, please do. Say something to grab their attention. You have the key to the best romance you covet. If you do nothing, chances are, nothing will happen.

Make your lover your priority number one.

*Love word for this Chapter* _____.

"Sharing food with another human being is an intimate act that should not be indulged in lightly," — M.F.K. Fisher

## 7 DINE TOGETHER OFTEN

People who dine together stay together and so do couples and lovers. During the lockdowns and even during stay-at-homes, it is important that couples learn the value of dining together.

Dining together has ten benefits for couples.

First, it cements and strengthens their bond. Food tastes good with love, smiles and laughter. During mealtimes, couples share just more than food; they share their love.

Second, it fortifies camaraderie. Being together at a meal works wonders on friendship. It is the best time to talk and ruminate over common interests. Friendships are cultivated and strengthened over food. As a couple, you can find the most appropriate time to discuss your love life and palatalize it with sumptuous meals.

Third, it accentuates comfort. Couples can sometimes get so engrossed into routines that they forget each other, literally. And the more they stay away from each other, the more uncomfortable they begin to feel in each other's presence. But at mealtimes, such discomfitures are broken and dismantled.

Fourth, it enthrones common space. Food is the most powerful healer of broken relationships. It is also usually the first place where love is hatched. It is no wonder that when couples first court (date) one another, they usually do it over a meal. This is because when people share meals, they are, indirectly, loosening up and inviting each other into their space. Love blooms and romance heightens in such moments.

Fifth, it promotes a common taste, literally. At the beginning, couples and lovers start to accept each other's food taste, and later, to appreciate their unique tastes in life. They also become familiar with each other's habits and mannerisms. All that happens when couples and lovers dine together.

Sixth, it revitalizes the romantic atmosphere. Many couples also found it easier to engage in physical contact after having a meal together. When they enjoy a meal together, they, implicitly, invite an atmosphere of physical touch. This accentuates their love life and may lead to unforgettable romance.

Seventh, it enhances openness and free expression. Fear of offending one another is reduced where couples eat and dine together. It also elevates a sense of freedom and diminishes chances of misunderstandings.

Eighth, food is synonymous with life, and couples who dine together also remain together in the relationship the longest.

Nineth, it brings joy. A partner who prepared the meal feels a sense of satisfaction when their lover enjoys the meal. They feel they are useful and loved. Or the partner who ordered the meal feels a sense of appreciativeness when the meal they ordered is enjoyed. There is something joy-bringing in lovers enjoying a meal together.

And tenth, as food is intrinsically satisfying, enjoying a meal together leads to a satisfying, romantic relationship. Life is satisfying with love and food.

And here are three reasons why food stimulates love and is stimulated by it in turn. First, food is a source of love. In every culture, people show that they care by giving strangers food. They show that they love someone and accept them by letting go of their most precious commodity – food.

Second, food is a source of life. When people share food, they are, in fact, sharing life. When lovers make love, they are equally sharing life.

And third, food is a source of enduring

friendship. Couples who begin as friends stick together even in troublesome times. They are able to survive because of friendship. Similarly, food connects people. When people share food, they are declaring in no uncertain terms that they are friends and not enemies. When couples dine together, it glorifies their friendship.

It is fine when lovers dine.

*Love word for this Chapter* _____.

> "It is an absolute human certainty that no one can know his own beauty or perceive a sense of his own worth until it has been reflected back to him in the mirror of another loving, caring human being" — John Joseph Powell

## 8 CULTIVATE INTIMACY

The Covid lockdowns and stay-at-home orders may also be the best time to cultivate the lovers' intimacy. Both men and women have roles to play. Both can do certain things to cultivate intimacy, even in Covid-19 pandemic times.

For men, here are ten things they can do: First, they can touch and fondle their wives and partners on consistent basis. They cannot give excuses anymore. They are "locked" together and are closer to each other. So, a timely hug, a part on the back and a spontaneous kiss or smooch, can do wonders. Women feel loved when they are touched in a non-sexual, loving and caring manner. Most women are put off by their partners because when their partner touches them, it is always when those partners want sex. To most women, sex is not the same as love.

Second, they can order or create some homemade trimmings for their wives or partners. To many women, sounds of love come in smaller bits. They are not all after Lamborghinis or Ferraris or Bentleys and expensive lingerie or perfumes. To most women, a man who goes into the neighborhood forest and brings them a wildflower, is a hero and a romantic guru.

Third, they can offer help with home chores, such as making the bed, doing laundry, cleaning the washrooms, decorating the backyard, washing dishes, volunteering to do grocery shopping or making lunch. There are one hundred and one ideas men can come up with to impress and "spoil" their women. All it takes is a caring thought and a creative stint.

Fourth, they can take care of the children while the woman is given a necessary break. Most women would love to see their men take the children away for a walk or play with them in the backyard. This may mean more, romantically, to a woman than saying meaningless words.

Fifth, whenever you can, work hard and give money to the woman so that she can spoil herself. With online shopping being commonplace during the pandemic, some money can go a long way to raise the lover's spirits.

Sixth, compliment the lover frequently. It is normal to feel "ashamed" to compliment a partner whom you live with permanently. It is easier for most men to heap compliments upon a temporary or prospective lover or for someone they want to win over. After they win her to themselves, they may stop complimenting her. But during the pandemic, you have another opportunity to find nice things about your lover and compliment her. And you don't need to go very far, begin with the make-up. Each time she makes up, say something nice.

Seventh, share in her joys. You can do things such as remembering her birthday or buying her flowers at Valentine's Day. You can also celebrate milestones like wedding anniversaries, and so on. All that shows that the romance is alive. It gives the woman hope for the future and faith in the relationship. Keeping quiet when you should be saying something, is not good for romance.

Eighth, depending on the nature of your friendship and romance and how your partner reacts to it, say as much "I love you," as it cannot be faked. What matters is that you mean what you say. If you don't mean it, don't say it. Saying empty "I love yous" pre-empts the meaning of real romance. The fact is that most women know when their partner is faking that they love those women.

Nineth, they can chide their partner in love. It is not always that stating your side is warranted. Sometimes a good and kind word, can go a long way in diffusing tensions. If your lover is irritable, try offering her massage. It could be just what she needs to calm down. And, of course, it is also romantic.

And tenth, they can start early to make sex moves. Most women would not be "in the mood" when they are tired or if the rest of the day were filled with hate and confrontations. However, most women find it easier and necessary to give themselves to a lover who has shown care and love throughout the day.

When it comes to men, women can do seven specific things to cultivate their love with them. First, they can showcase confidence in their men. There is nothing a man appreciates more than a woman who shows respect and mutual submission to him.

Second, they can be humble, even when they are smarter than their men or make more money than their men do. A wise woman knows when to challenge their husband. If it can be misunderstood, a wise woman will wait for a right time.

Third, they can avoid confrontations, even if they are right. This may seem masculine, but it is a truism. Most men will not be comfortable living under the same roof with a confrontational and voluble woman. During the pandemic when families are expected to remain together, this quality is even more vital. The best time to confront a man is during love-making. At that time, men's defences are weak, and the likelihood that they will change for the better are heightened.

Fourth, they can break the silence. Majority of men would want to make love to their partners every day. But practical realities may inhibit the women from engaging in sex, daily. However, most men would appreciate a lover who initiates the love moves. Women should do this more frequently. The feeling is akin to when men lovingly compliment their women after making up.

Fifth, they can tell the men that they love them. When men say, "I love you," and women respond, "And me, too," or "I love you, too," it demoralizes men. It sounds more stimuli than hearty. During the Covid pandemic, a woman can do her romance a favor by being the first to tell her lover or spouse, "I love you."

Sixth, they can forgive often. No woman is able to engage in meaningful sex with their partner with unforgiveness. Although this also applies to men, it is more devasting to women. Like their genitalia or anatomy symbolizes, women feel things "inside" while men "outside." One shocking or pleasurable event may end right there for men, but for women, it may just be the beginning. This is the reason why they seldom forget a man who makes good love to them, but they don't forget the one who made it worse, either. However, with the exercising of unconditional forgiveness to their lover, women can free themselves up to have good moments with their spouses. This is even more important during the lockdowns and stay-at-home orders than at any other moment in time.

Forgiveness gives the woman the power to enjoy her spouse or lover's company. It empowers her to take their romance to another level. But as long as she is not willing to forgive, any encounter with her man is only theater. Forgiveness is a two-edged sword; it gives spiritual invisibility and it ignites a passionate flame towards a fulfilled romantic and sexual life.

And seventh, they can take time to understand their men. One of the problems why relationships fail, is because of negligence. Although this may go either way, a woman's negligence of her man's sexual desires is more traumatic and devasting than the woman's. This is not to say that men should neglect the sexual needs of their women, no.

Some men can rarely survive without sex; most women can. There are exceptions, of course. One of the reasons why men marry is sex. Most married men rarely leave their matrimonial bed if they are sexually satisfied. Delving "outside" is rarely for love, but for sex. A wise woman will ensure that her man has "food" at home. And if men are not "starved" sexually at home, they will rarely go out for other females. They will also be less likely to engage in pornography.

This does not imply that men should be careless and should not exercise self-control. Even when they are "starved," men should remain faithful to their women and find creative ideas to engage. In the end, it will pay dividends.

Love done is better than love said.

*Love word for this Chapter* _____.

"Encouragement requires empathy and seeing the world from your spouse's perspective. We must first learn what is important to our spouse. Only then can we give encouragement. With verbal encouragement, we are trying to communicate, 'I know. I care. I am with you. How can I help?' We are trying to show that we believe in [them] and in [their] abilities. We are giving credit and praise" – Gary Chapman.

## 9 FINE-TUNE YOUR LOVE LANGUAGE

Love has a language. The longer couples stay together, the easier they begin to understand each other's love language. There are two types of love languages, the spoken language and the non-verbal language.

Spoken language is cultivated first. It is vocalized through words. This entails communication. During the Covid pandemic, good communication between couples and lovers can enhance their love relationships. When couples and lovers talk to each other freely, they can accomplish a great deal for their love relationship. Verbal communication must be accompanied by feedback. Where only one partner speaks and the other one listens only, there will be problems. It is better to say everything in a partner's mind than to bottle up with concerns and hate. But it is far better to say what is on one's mind with self-control and in love. Couples should try not to say anything when they are angry. A right word at the right time has the potential to heal a relationship and strengthen romantic love.

During the lockdowns, it is vital for couples to learn to talk to each other frequently and openly. This is especially advisable to those couples who live under the same roof. Open communication can ease up emotions and resolve conflicts and lessen disagreements during the Covid-19 pandemic.

The other type of love language can be accomplished non-verbally. This also might include implied language. Couples should be sensitive to one another. They should be able to "read" and "hear" correctly their lovers' non-verbal language. Couples should be able to know when their partner is tired, afraid, sad, happy, concerned or needs attention without uttering any words.

Among the best love languages to cultivate, verbally and non-verbally, are the following:

Couples and lovers should learn to how to use the "You language." The next notes are taken from the author's website (charlesmwewa.com).

"The 'You' Language": Why don't you say, "You're my everything," rather than, "I am your everything." The "You Language" places the emphasis on the object of love rather than its subject. You're its subject. When lovers see that you put them as a priority, they are most likely to reciprocate. In conflict resolution, tensions tend to increase where one lover keeps defending their position. Well, you can still defend your position by deflecting blame from your spouse, for example, instead of saying, "You're always offending me," rather say, "I think there is something offensive about your language." In that way, you deflect the blame and at the same time allow for discussion or even introspection.

The secret is in this: When it comes to praising your spouse or partner, say, "You," but if you should want to cast blame, say, "I." "I am of the view that your previous statement to me was offensive," rather than, "You are offensive, I hate it." When lovers or partners feel that you have intruded into their wisdom or comfortable space, they will react in defiance, and even use derogatory language.

Language is the primary avenue for communication. And choice of the right language use and response is key to a relatively peaceful and romantic or love relationship. Consider a partner who says, "You are a liar, a cheater." Well, there is no more room left for discussion, isn't it? You have already judged your partner, and it can almost be guaranteed that the response will be defensive. Why? Because you have already judged them. What if you said, "I think that you cheated on me." Indeed, you have left room for discussion and even settling the dispute. Consider how many times you may have shut your partner or spouse off, because you left them with no chance to respond.

We can learn a few things from the legal profession. In what is known as pleadings, it is against the rules of advocacy to plead the law or the evidence. You're required to plead only material facts. And the reason is that, if you plead law or evidence first, you give no room for defence. In other words, you pre-empt the defendant or accused from ever advancing a defence. In law, they say, you have erased an "air of reality" to the potential defence. A good judge will pour scorn on your defence. It is because judges understand that no matter how egregious some allegations may sound, there is always an explanation. Just as it is unjust to judge and sentence someone for the unproved allegations, it is also not good to judge your spouse or lover before they present their side of the story.

Similarly, in relationships, bad things will happen (if they haven't happened yet, it is just a matter of time). There will be moments of disagreements, of misunderstandings and of fear and enmity. These are bound to happen. And it is not the question of "if" but one of "when." The best relationships, romances and marriages are framed from the ashes of trouble, disagreements and even close-break-ups. But "how" the couple resolved the conflict is what mattered. If you want to run away from the first hint of trouble, know that you are only postponing trouble. It's likely all your subsequent relationships will end badly because you have not resolved the core flaw.

There is no "perfect" relationship, at least as of now. Good relationships become – in other words, they were made by compromise, forgiveness, and even by some degree of madness. By that is meant using language to defuse tensions. For example, it will sound foolish to say, "I think that Juliet is in love with you." Rather than, "You're in love with Juliet, I know it." Well, the poor fellow will not know how to answer. And if not handled properly, you would have pushed the lover towards Juliet.

It is the same for the ladies. If you tell your lover, "You're not a real man, in fact, I know that you don't love me." Well, what options does the guy have; probably not even a recantation will save the relationship. But if you had said, "I believe that you're a real man, but, presently, I don't see you manifesting that. This is leading me to thinking that you probably don't love me."

You see, you strike a sympathetic tone, and a wise guy will be deeply repentant after hearing that. He would want to live up to your appreciation and positive view of him. The result will be rekindled love, romance, and a thriving relationship.

Try these tips for a month and see the results.

The other love languages to develop and embrace during the Covid-19 pandemic in relationships may include: The "I am sorry" language; the "Please" language; the "Forgive or pardon me" language; the "Thank you" language; the "After you" language; and the "I love you" language. Couples and lovers who say these words frequently and consistently enjoy romance very much as well.

Love language is relationship's bandage.

*Love word for this Chapter* _____.

"Sex is more than an act of pleasure, it's the ability to be able to feel so close to a person, so connected, so comfortable that it's almost breathtaking to the point you feel you can't take it. And at this moment you're a part of them" – Thom York.

## 10 MAKE LOVE OFTEN

Make love often and have sex less. This may sound like a cliché, but many couples rarely make love. What they call love-making is a quick attempt at feeling good, usually at the expense of the other partner. Love-making takes time and preparation. All conditions must be right for both lovers. If only one lover is prepared and the other is not, what the duo did might be called sex but not love-making.

Love-making requires being sensitive to the needs of the other party. It involves taking time to appreciate and "worship" all the little elements that make up the other lover. It cannot be a sharp-shoot without counting the totality of the shot. Most of what is called love-making just targets the "center" without first taking time to offer homage to the neighbors. The exercise may relax one but leave the other totally feeling used, and sometimes even feeling abused.

There is, therefore, no better time to relax, take time and embrace the moment than during the pandemic when life seems to be slower. Couples and lovers should take time and give to each other the gift of love-making without pressure, frustration or a sense of duty. And as mentioned in Chapter 8, the cultivation of intimacy must precede the act of love-making.

Love-making is both art and science. It is both easy and complex. It is both satisfying and frustrating. It is both a blessing and a curse. It is both sacred and sinful. It is the tendency the lovers have and the attitude they attach to it that will make one and not the other or both.

As an art, it takes practice to augment its complex facets. It takes time and patience to harness its honey and plum its efficacies. As art, it requires human creative skill and fond imagination – to leave a unique and lasting impression on the other. Size and shape do not matter. What matters is how and what you do with the assets available, and most humans have these assets. Everyone may make babies but not everyone can make love. It takes one's full concentration and discernment to satisfy the sexual needs of the other person. Failure to capture this imagination, makes sex a drudge.

As a science, love-making is not made in a vacuum or on a template. It requires an understanding of human anatomy – what matters to the human sexual aggrandizement and experience. Love-making must be empowering and not overpowering. It must inspire love and not conjure up hate disguised as a love feeling. When love-making is done drudgingly, it becomes a burden and not a pleasure, leading, especially women, to the feeling that they have been used or abused. Those who take time and knowledge to understand what makes their partner "enjoy" the act, will do sex less and make love more. Love-making should not be menial labor; it must be a pleasant work.

Those who know and understand their partner (which come with time and patience) can be assured that their love-making will be relatively easy, satisfying, a blessing, and sacred. People say, "They have good chemistry" and by this they mean that such lovers are capable of creating orgasmic reactions. It is true, but it is also dangerous to rely on the orgasmic reaction as a measure of good sex. For sure, one partner can easily reach orgasm or have multiple of them at the expense of the other. (Some people may do this using sex toys). What constitutes good sex is the ability to offer oneself unselfishly to the other, even to the point of "sacrificing" themselves for the other. As the good old golden saying goes, "Do unto others as you would have them do unto you." There is no better place to apply this benevolence than to love-making.

Love your partner as you love yourself.

# INDEX

abused, 34, 35
advocacy, 30
allegations, 30
anatomy, 23, 35
anniversaries, 21
appreciates, 22
appreciativeness, 17
art, 34
ashes, 31
assets, 34
attention, 14, 28
attitude, 34
backyard, 20
bed, 20, 24
benevolence, 36
Bentleys, 20
birthday, 21
blessing, 34, 35
blissful future, 9
bond of love, 6
break-ups, 5, 31
burden, 35
businesses, 5
camaraderie, 15
career goals, 7
cheater, 30
children, 20
comfort, 16, 29
communication, 27, 28, 29
company, 24
complement, 21, 23
compliment, 21

confidence, 22
conflict resolution, 29
confrontations, 22
couple, 3, 15, 31
courage, 9
Covid, 1, 3, 4, 5, 8, 9, 10, 11, 12, 13, 19, 23, 27, 28, 32
creative, 12, 20, 34
cultivate, 1, 5, 19, 22, 28
curse, 34
defence, 30
defendant, 30
degree, 8
depression, 5
derogatory, 29
dine, 15, 16, 17, 18
diploma, 8
discussion, 29, 30
dishes, 20
distress, 5
dreams, 9
duty, 34
education, 7
endurance, 13
enmity, 31
eternity, 10
faith, 1, 2, 21
families, 5, 23
favor, 23
fear, 1, 2, 9, 12, 31
feedback, 28

feeling good, 33
females, 25
Ferraris, 20
food, 15, 16, 17, 24
freedom, 17
friendship, 15, 18, 21
frustrations, 12
genitalia, 23
gory, 10
graduate studies, 8
grocery, 20
happiness, 9
happy, 6, 28
harmony, 3
hate, 12, 13, 22, 28, 29, 35
healer, 16
hobbies, 7
homage, 34
honey, 34
hope, 7, 8, 9, 21
hopelessness, 10
hug, 12, 19
humble, 22
husband, 22
I love you, 21, 23, 32
imagination, 9, 34
in death, 4
in life, 4, 16
infected, 1, 3
inspiration, 9
interests, 14, 15
introspection, 29
job, 8
joy, 9, 10, 17
judge, 30
Juliet, 31
kiss, 12, 19

knowledge, 35
labor, 35
Lamborghinis, 20
language, 27, 28, 29, 31, 32
laughter, 15
laundry, 20
law, 30
lingerie, 20
lockdowns, 1, 5, 8, 15, 19, 24, 28
locked-up, 2
love life, 1, 11, 16
love-making, 23, 33, 34, 35
lovers, 3, 4, 5, 10, 15, 16, 17, 18, 19, 27, 28, 29, 32, 33, 34, 35
lunch, 20
mannerisms, 16
marriages, 5, 31
masculine, 22
masks, 2
material facts, 30
meals, 16
mealtimes, 15, 16
memories, 4
mind, 28
misunderstandings, 3, 17, 31
money, 20, 22
mood, 22
moves, 22, 23
negligence, 13, 24
news, 1, 2, 3, 12
newspapers, 3
non-sexual, 20
openness, 17
orgasm, 35

orgasmic reaction, 35
pandemic, 1, 3, 4, 7, 8, 9,
  10, 13, 19, 20, 21, 22,
  23, 27, 28, 32, 34
paradise, 6
partner, 4, 11, 12, 17, 20,
  21, 22, 23, 28, 29, 30,
  33, 35, 36
passions, 7
patience, 34, 35
perfumes, 20
physical contact, 16
pleasurable, 23
pornography, 13, 25
pre-Covid, 2, 8, 9
priority, 13, 14, 29
procrastinate, 8
quarrels, 3
radios, 3
regret, 4, 11
relationships, 1, 16, 24, 30,
  31, 32
remote learning, 8
repentant, 32
respect, 22
restrictions, 4
romance, 14, 16, 17, 21,
  23, 24, 28, 32
roof, 22, 28
satisfaction, 17
science, 34, 35
seven specific things, 22
sex, 20, 22, 23, 24, 33, 35
sexual life, 24
sexual needs, 24, 35

share, 15, 16, 17, 18, 21
shopping, 20
skill, 34
smarter, 22
smiles, 15
smirk, 19
sorrow, 9
sorry, 32
source, 17
stay-at-home, 5, 8, 24
stress, 5
submission, 22
tastes, 16
ten things, 19
tensions, 22, 29, 31
Thank you, 32
till death do us part, 4
tomorrow, 7, 8, 9, 10
trouble, 31
TV, 3
uncomfortable, 16
unconditional forgiveness,
  24
vacuum, 35
Valentine's Day, 21
video games, 9
warmth, 7
washrooms, 20
website, 29
wedding, 21
wildflower, 20
wives, 19, 20
work, 20, 35
worship, 33

## ABOUT THE AUTHOR

## CHARLES MWEWA

Charles Mwewa (LLM – cand.) is a Dad, a husband, a prolific author and researcher, poet, novelist, political thinker, a law professor, and Christian and community leader. Mwewa has written no less than 30 books and counting. Mwewa, his wife and their three daughters, reside in the Canadian Capital City of Ottawa.

# AUTHOR'S CONTACT

Email Address: spynovel2016@gmail.com

Facebook: https://www.facebook.com/charlesmwewa

Twitter: https://twitter.com/BooksMwewa

Instagram: https://www.instagram.com/mwewabooks/?hl=en

Author's Website: https://www.charlesmwewa.com

www.ingramcontent.com/pod-product-compliance
Lightning Source LLC
LaVergne TN
LVHW010027070426
835510LV00001B/15